KEEPING A PONY
AT GRASS

Written for the Pony Club Organization Committee

by

MRS. O. FAUDEL-PHILLIPS F.I.H.

Illustrations by Joan Wanklyn

A PONY CLUB PUBLICATION

Published by

THE BRITISH HORSE SOCIETY

NATIONAL EQUESTRIAN CENTRE

KENILWORTH, WARWICKSHIRE, CV8 2LR.

Printed in England by
Northbourne Press Limited, Coventry

FOREWORD

BY

BRIAN VESEY-FITZGERALD

I spend a great deal of my life with animals of one kind or another, and most of my spare time reading books about animals and their care. It is very rarely indeed that I come across an author who has had the courage to set forth in plain terms in the introduction to his book precisely what he intends to do in the book itself. Not only has Olive Faudel-Phillips done this, but — and I should doubt if this has ever happened before — she has fulfilled her intentions to the letter !

We are, as everyone knows, a nation of animal-lovers. But we have some of the oddest ideas about animals. This is because we are very inclined to allow sentiment to overrule common sense.

Ponies are individuals, just as humans are. They can be happy or sad, self-sufficient or lonely. But they cannot express their feelings as humans can. The true animal-lover (and this applies equally to the good pony-owner, of course) not only takes care of the animal's physical needs, but also attempts to understand the animal's mind. It is only thus that you can get a true relationship.

And this is precisely what Olive Faudel-Phillips does. She not only loves and understands ponies and their care, she — and I hope that she will take this as a great compliment — thinks like a pony. Which is what every pony-owner should try to do. Be that as it may, there can be no doubt that whatever anyone can possibly want to know about keeping a pony at grass, it is here in this book. Every pony-owner will be the better for it. And so will every pony, which is really much more important.

Two other important Pony Club Publications are

"The Manual of Horsemanship"

and

The Instructor's Handbook

These are the Official Handbooks of the
British Horse Society and the Pony Club

Both obtainable from the British Horse Society
National Equestrian Centre, Kenilworth,
Warwickshire, CV8 2LR.

CONTENTS

ILLUSTRATIONS

INTRODUCTION

This book is written to help members, their parents and their ponies.

TO HELP PONY OWNERS to keep their pony fit and well all the year round.

TO HELP PONIES.

HOW TO BUDGET.

HOW TO COPE with some of the problems.

HOW TO AVOID some of the difficulties that may occur.

ABOVE ALL it is intended to dispel the bogy that just because one has a field a pony can automatically live in it.

Ponies are happy and contented at grass and will give of their best, be it out hunting (Fig. 1), rallies, rides, or whatever their work, provided their few wants are attended to regularly and consistently.

HUNTISBEARE 1966   O.F-P.

Fig. 1. Ponies will give of their best, be it out hunting

CHAPTER I

WILD PONIES

Ponies who have unlimited range, for example in the New Forest, on Dartmoor and on the Welsh Hills, may be able to live all the year round without human help. They are in small herds in their natural surroundings (Fig. 2), seeking water, food and shelter.

Fig. 2.   On the Welsh hills in their natural surroundings

Their feet keep naturally trimmed by the wear they get. The grease in their ungroomed coats turns the rain, keeps them warm and is a protection from flies.

On the other hand a pony turned out in a field cannot live without regular attention all the year round. It has a large part of its freedom taken away. It can only drink and eat what it finds in that field. There may or may not be any shelter and the range being restricted, its feet will not keep naturally trimmed.

CHAPTER 2

FIELDS

Things to know about :

Water. It is essential for ponies to have a plentiful supply of clean water so that they can drink as and when they want. The most natural and the best is a running stream or a pond with a spring in it. A stagnant pond silted up with mud is not good—an alternative water supply must be provided.

Fig. 3.   Moorland pond and stream

Some fields have piped water and troughs (Fig. 4). It is wiser to have one of the cattle troughs which are specially fitted with a ball-cock so that each time ponies or cattle drink, the trough automatically refills itself. The ball-cock is enclosed in its own covered box so that animals cannot interfere with it. Even so, it must be looked at once a week. Grit or weeds may get in, causing it to choke

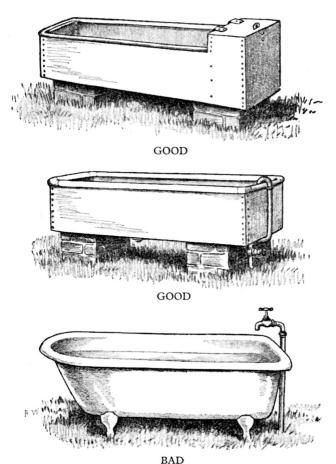

GOOD

GOOD

BAD

Fig. 4. Water Troughs

Fig. 5. Gates tied up with string are not signs that you care—avoid using a bath—tins, litter, bits of wire

and flood, or something may·be wrong with the water supply which prevents the trough from filling properly.

Avoid using an old bath for a trough (Figs. 4 & 5) ; unfortunately they are seen too often in fields. They spoil the look of a field and the sharp sides can give a pony a nasty cut or bruise.

If there is no water supply in the field then water has to be taken daily by hand.

Whatever container is used it must be firmly placed so that the pony cannot knock it over when it is half empty. All troughs should be emptied and scrubbed out at least four times a year.

Gates MUST open wide and shut properly and MUST have a secure catch. Gates tied up with string or looped round with wire are not signs of good horsemastership, or that you care much whether your pony gets out or strays on a road (Fig. 5).

There is a simple inexpensive galvanised non-sag gate hook on the market which the cleverest pony will not undo.

Fences. A post and rails fence is the best and is the right kind of artificial fencing for horses and ponies (Figs. 6 & 34). It is very expensive but it is safe and lasts for years. Posts and wire are more often used but do not last so long. This is a cheap form of fencing and alright while the wire is taut and the posts firm. Old wire fences can be very dangerous (Fig. 7). Wire fences must be kept in good repair to be safe. Barbed wire is very dangerous.

Hedges, walls, and banks (Figs 10, 12 & 16), which are the natural kinds of fencing for different parts of the country, are all good if kept well maintained. There must be no weak places for ponies to push through. Gaps mended with bits of wire, a single thin rail or some dead branches soon become gaps again. In spring and autumn, when ponies are changing their coats, they will rub against any convenient post, rail or the gate.

Inspect all fences regularly.

Fig. 6.   A post and rails fence is best

Shelter is essential in winter from rain and wind—in summer from sun and flies. It can be a building or a shed, a high stout hedge or shady trees (Fig. 10).

(Figs. 6 & 8). An open-fronted shed is good—a shed with only one doorway or with narrow doorways (Fig. 9) is bad because two ponies may get squeezed going out quickly. Many a pony is shy and afraid of being kicked or bullied by another pony. It will not use a shed unless it has a wide open front, i.e., three sides closed and the whole of the fourth side open.

Fig. 7.   Old wire fences are very dangerous

It is often noticed that some ponies will not use their shed during the worst winter weather, but in summer, when it is hot and the flies drive them nearly mad, they will take refuge in the shed.

Ponies rarely lie down in their shed, under trees or close to a hedge ; more often they will take advantage of a slight fold in the ground which gives shelter from wind when they are lying down.

(Fig. 10). A high deep and stout hedge is good and gives shelter in all weathers besides acting as a wind break. Banks and walls protect from rain and wind but not always from the sun.

(Fig. 10). Shady trees in summertime protect from sun and flies and ponies will stand under them, usually head to tail. Trees in winter-time (Fig. 16), without their leaves, do not offer much protection. Small thickets, bushy hollies, clumps of evergreen shrubs or a small wood or spinney are all places where ponies can shelter in rough weather.

Fig. 8.   An open-fronted shed is good

Inspection. Fields need regularly inspecting all over and round the fences for bottles, tins and litter (Fig. 5), especially from Easter to October. A wire fence may have been climbed through and the wire become loose—there may even be loose bits of wire about (Fig. 7).

Look out for any holes and fill in with stones and earth. Stamp them well in.

Old dead branches sticking out at eye level can be dangerous and should be broken or sawn off close to the tree. In fact it is a good thing to get into the habit of noticing anything in a field that may cause a pony to get hurt or caught up.

Look round the hedges for the poisonous plants (Fig. 11), Deadly Nightshade, Ragwort and for Yew. Pull up by the roots the two former. Remove from the field and burn them. It is the dead or

Fig. 9. Narrow doorways are bad

half-dead branches and bits of Yew and Ragwort that are so deadly poisonous to ponies and cattle.

Grazing. Ponies will only graze the grasses that they like. They will starve rather than eat rank, tufty grass or the sour grass round their own droppings. Therefore a pony cannot live continually in the same field. It must be rested periodically and have some treatment.

Grass first begins to grow very slowly in April. It is at its best from mid-May until early July. By October the goodness has gone out of the grass and it has stopped growing.

Fields soon become "horse-sick" if continually grazed or over-grazed by ponies. The ill effect of red worm are greatly increased if fields are grazed too long without being properly dressed and ested.

Fig. 10.   High stout hedge gives shelter in all weathers

Young ponies do not do well on lime-starved land although older ponies may (Fig. 12).

If ponies start gnawing bark off trees it is a sign that something is lacking in their diet. By always keeping a large lump of rock salt in the field the risk of ponies barking the trees will be lessened.

Fig. 11. Yew. Deadly Nightshade

Care of Grass : Sharing a Field with Cattle. This is one of the best ways to keep a field evenly grazed and the grass sweet. The cattle will pull off the rough, longer grasses.

Having two fields is ideal—then each field can be rested in turn and receive proper treatment.

Electric fencing, as a temporary fence in the spring, enables a field to be grazed evenly by giving the grass in the rested part a chance to grow. Be sure to lead a pony up and show it this fencing the first time it is used (Fig. 13).

Fig. 12.   Young ponies do not do so well on lime-starved land

Important. Do not forget about water and shelter with this strip graziug.

Droppings. Horse and pony droppings should be regularly picked up from any field (Fig. 14). Using a pair of boards or small shovel and a barrow, wheel the droppings away to a manure heap or

Fig. 13. Be sure to lead a pony up and show it this fencing

Fig. 14.   Droppings should be regularly picked up

the garden compost heap. If it is not possible to pick up the droppings then they must be scattered with a wire rake once a week (Fig. 15).

Fields need attention at certain seasons, year in and year out, so seek the advice of a farmer neighbour about how to care for your field ; when to harrow and roll ; what with and when to dress the field ; when to have a cutter run over the field to keep down thistles, long weeds and rough rank grasses ; when and how to cut and trim the hedges and cut brambles and nettles (Fig. 16).

It is worth taking a little trouble and care so that your pony can get the best grazing out of every square yard of a field.

Fig. 15.   Wire rake

Fig. 16. Care for your field. Cut and trim the hedges

CHAPTER 3

FEEDING

All the best grass and food in the world is no good to a pony unless it always has a plentiful supply of clean water.

Ponies need a lot of bulky food all the year round to keep them fit and well. Lack of enough bulk, or roughage, as it is sometimes called, is very often the cause of a pony being in poor condition.

Ponies do most of their grazing from dawn to dusk, so it is easy to remember that as Autumn turns to Winter with less daylight, the pony has less time in which to eat enough grass to last it through the long hours of darkness. There is less grass, and therefore less bulk, from October to April.

Food has to do many things for a pony. These are the main ones :

> Keep the pony alive ; keep it warm ; keep it in good condition with a shine on its coat ; give it enough energy to do all the work required of it.

Therefore one must continually be thinking whether one's pony has a regular supply and enough of the right kind of food.

What to Feed. Extra food is given to ponies in two ways, each for a different reason.

1 *Hay*—which is the bulky and filling-up feed.
2 *Short Feed*—(oats, horsenuts, etc.), which is concentrated and is the sustaining, warmth and energy-making feed.

If, for various reasons, you can only give one kind of extra food, then give the pony hay. Plenty of really good, clean, sweet-smelling hay, and you will not go far wrong.

Meadow hay or seed hay—ponies like and will do well on either but good quality it must be. Never buy bad quality hay ; the price is just the same and it will cost more in the long run. It is bad for the pony and much of it is wasted, so insist on getting really good hay.

A short feed can consist of any, or a mixture of anv, of the following :

    Oats, whole or bruised; Horse or Pony Nuts, Beans, cracked or split ; Flaked Maize.

Fig. 17.   It is wiser not to give oats to very small ponies

These can be fed neat but it is not so good for a pony. If possible a good big double handful of chaff should be mixed in to make the pony eat slower and chew more.

Bran alone has not much food value for a pony at grass, as it tends to go straight through ; but it can be used dry instead of chaff if there is difficulty in getting chaff.

It is wiser not to give oats, beans or maize to very small ponies (Figs. 17 & 20) ; they usually do well on hay alone (Fig. 19). If they must be given a short feed give horsenuts, mixed with either chaff or bran.

The same applies to giving extra food for an excitable, hot pony. Good rarely comes of cutting out its food altogether and the pony will only lose condition. Feed horsenuts or silcocks, neither of which will excite a pony, and feed plenty of hay.

When to Feed. The right time to give food to ponies at grass is at dawn and again about an hour before dusk. Give some hay in the morning as soon as it is light. The rest of the hay and the short feed should be given in the afternoon. In this way the pony will get the best advantage from the food during the coldest part of the twenty-four hours.

These times are not always possible but do feed, or ask whoever is going to do it, to arrange so that the pony is fed, at the same time every day. THIS IS IMPORTANT. All animals respond to regular hours and seem to possess a clock in their heads. The pony will be waiting at the gate. If two or more ponies are turned out together they will soon begin milling round and trouble starts if they are kept waiting (Fig. 18), so always be particular to feed at regular times every day.

Some people give an extra feed occasionally or only if the pony is being ridden or worked. This may be all right when there is enough grass, but in winter it is both unfair and bad for a pony, which cannot understand being fed one day and not the next. When the pony needs extra food, feed regularly and consistently.

Over the four seasons of a year let us consider which months ponies need, and do not need, extra food. Remember there can be no hard and fast rule. Circumstances must always govern each

Fig. 18.   Trouble starts if they are kept waiting

pony ; its field, its work, and whether it lives North, South, East or West, in a town or in the country.

May and June. The grass is growing and has its full feed value. Ponies can eat all the food and bulk they need and, in addition, they can make good the condition they have lost during the winter, and the earlier months of the year. A pony should fill out, get a gloss on its coat ; be given the chance to pick up and be worked as little as possible. It should not need any extra food.

July to November. On average grazing a pony should be able to live without extra feeding except during the holidays. Doing an average summer holiday programme a pony will need a short feed daily. It will do many days with long hours out of its field, so the concentrated short feed will keep it going during those hours. It will catch up with its bulk food because it can graze during most of the summer nights.

November to Mid-December. Unless on very good grazing, a pony will need hay once a day, and a daily short feed if being hunted.

Mid-December to April. Ponies must now be fed hay once or twice daily. Definitely twice daily during frost or snow. If a pony is being hunted then it must have a daily short feed as well as hay.

Thinking ahead, as one must always do with the care and feeding of animals, we want our pony to be fit and well for the Easter holidays (often one of the busiest) so give a good short feed as well as hay daily from December to April. As winter turns to Spring ponies feel at their lowest. They have used up all their surplus fat. They will soon be changing their coats. The grass has not begun to grow, so that daily extra short feed will really help the pony.

Year-at-a-Glance. Showing approximately which months to give hay and short feed.

Month	Hay	Short Feed
January	Yes	Yes
February	Yes	Yes
March	Yes	Yes
April	Yes	Yes
May	No	No
June	No	No
July	No	No
August	No	Perhaps
September	No	Perhaps
October	Perhaps	No
November	Perhaps	Perhaps
December	Yes	Yes

Fig. 20.   Very small pony

Haynets are usually in three sizes (Fig. 19) :

Large : (Hunter) holding 10 to 12 lb. of hay when stuffed
COMPLETELY full

Medium : (Cob and Pony) 7 to 8 lb. of hay when stuffed
COMPLETELY full.

Small : (very small ponies) up to 3 lb. of hay when stuffed
COMPLETELY full.

Buy tarred haynets—they last much longer.

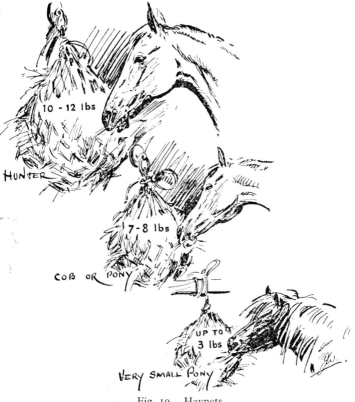

Fig. 19. Haynets

Hay. Budget for the quantity needed for the winter and allow a margin in case there is a long frost or the pony needs extra hay.

A pony eating two medium sized nets of hay a day will need one ton of good quality hay for 18 to 20 weeks. If the hay is only moderate quality then more will be needed.

Short Feed. How to budget for quantities :

A pony having about 4 lb. a day of either horse or pony nuts, bruised or whole oats, will need one cwt. bag a month.

If a big double handful of chaff is mixed with each feed then allow two large sacks of chaff a month.

If $1\frac{1}{2}$ to 2 lb. of bran is used instead of chaff then allow $\frac{1}{2}$ cwt. of bran a month.

From these quantities it should be easy to work out approximately how much food will be needed and what will be the cost of the pony's keep.

Fig. 21.   Large dust bins with lids are good

Ponies, like humans, vary in how much and what they eat and no rule can be laid down. Observe the pony and learn from it.

Storage. All forage must be stored in a clean dry place, free from rats and from access by chickens, dogs and the rest. Large dust bins with lids are good for keeping horsenuts, oats, etc. in (Fig. 21).

If the field where the pony is turned out is some distance from the house it may be necessary to have a dry place near the field in which to store hay and feed.

How to give Short Feed. It is wasteful to throw a feed down on the bare ground and not possible to do so in wet weather. Some container must be provided (Fig. 22). A feed box made of wood or galvanised iron is good—one for each pony and placed on the ground wide apart, out of kicking range.

Fig. 22   Feed boxes—portable manger

There are portable galvanised mangers made with two big hooks to hang on to a stout rail in a fence (Fig. 22). If a feed box is home-made be sure it is very strong and that there are no splinters.

If one pony has to have a special feed or an extra feed then take that pony out of the field, out of sight of the other ponies, to feed it.

Fig. 23.   Right

How to give Hay. Hay put on the ground is rather wasteful. Ponies pick out the best, treading and spoiling the rest. If there are a number of ponies turned out together this may be the only way. If so, be sure to put the heaps on a big circle, each heap wide apart from the last so that ponies cannot kick each other. Put one extra heap to the number of ponies. There will be less squabbling and it insures the shy pony getting its share.

Hay fed in haynets is excellent (Fig. 19). Any not eaten will remain clean and above the muddy ground. The ponies are able to return and eat when they want to. There must be a haynet for each pony in the field. Haynets must be tied very firmly to a strong fence (Fig. 6) or tree and high enough so that the pony does not catch a foot in it (Figs. 23 & 24). A haynet sags lower as it empties. Place haynets well apart to prevent biting and kicking.

Fig. 24. Wrong

Wooden hayracks as used by cattle are good.

The ground will get poached in wet weather wherever ponies are fed so it may be necessary to use different parts of a field or fence if this is practical.

CHAPTER 4

PONIES IN FROST AND SNOW

The water supply, whether trough or pond, must have the ice broken at least three times a day. A pony is unable to break even thin ice by itself.

Fig. 25. Ponies do not mind cold, dry weather

Additional hay as well as the pony's daily supply must be given during frost or snow as these put a stop to any grazing. Ponies do not necessarily mind very cold dry weather (Fig. 25) ; what they hate is cold, wet weather and wind.

It is very important to go on feeding when the thaw sets in, it is often wet and cold ; what grass there is is soggy and shrivelled.

When the ground is frozen and there is no give in it, it is very rough for an unshod pony. The horn may crack and bits break off. This may not happen if the ponies are shod. In either case when it thaws look out for a bruised sole or bruised heels.

CHAPTER 5

ABOUT FEET AND SHOES

"No foot—no 'oss"—Mr. Jorrocks has handed down to us no truer words. We shall do well never to forget them. A pony with feet and shoes regularly cared for will go a long way to giving 100 per cent. performance. It is neither safe nor fair on the pony to ride it when the feet or shoes need attention.

Fig. 26.   Horn growing over—risen clenches

Overgrown, split and cracked horn, worn, loose or twisted shoes, risen clenches (Fig. 26), horn growing over the shoe and the shoe pressing into the foot or heels (Fig. 37)—these will cause a pony discomfort and pain ; they may also cause brushing, faulty action and stumbling. So it is important for ponies, from the time they are foals and for the rest of their lives, to pay that regular visit to the farrier every four to six weeks. That is, eight to thirteen times a year (Fig. 27).

Fig. 27. Visit the farrier every four to six weeks

It does not necessarily mean a new set of shoes each visit. The amount of road work, the pony's conformation and its action are what govern the length of time a set of shoes will last.

The farrier may take off the shoes, re-shape them, trim the feet and put the shoes on again with new nails. This is called "a remove."

If a pony is unshod the farrier will trim the horn to keep the foot a good shape and the right length (Fig. 28).

If a pony is not going to be ridden in term time, then at the end of the holidays it is wise to ask the farrier for his advice. He may suggest removing all four shoes and leaving the pony unshod. He may put tips on the fore feet and leave the hind feet unshod. A tip prevents the toe from cracking and bits breaking off if the ground is hard in winter or summer (Fig. 29).

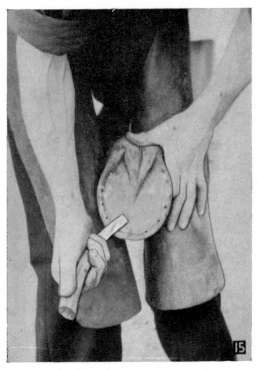

Fig. 28.   Trim the horn

Anyone at boarding school must make arrangements with the farrier to attend to the pony's feet once, at least, during term time, whether the pony's shoes are left on or taken off.

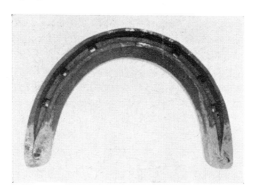

Fig. 29. A tip prevents the toe from cracking

In both "The Manual of Horsemanship" and the Pony Club Film Strip lecture and book, "The Foot and Shoeing," there are full details and a wealth of information on Feet, Shoes and Shoeing.

CHAPTER 6

CATCHING UP AND TURNING OUT

Ponies need catching frequently. Some ponies are never difficult to catch—others remain shy all their lives. There is many a pony who will not let a grown-up catch it.

Get a shy pony into the habit of coming to a call, letting it link up the voice with a tit-bit. Ponies love bread. NEVER give sugar. It leads to nipping, jealousy, not being caught, and a host of other bad habits.

Fig. 30. Always put the rope round the neck behind the pony's ears

Young or shy ponies prefer to be gently scratched or rubbed on the shoulder or neck rather than patted.

Slip a piece of rope or string round a pony's neck on each visit to the field, whether it is intended to catch the pony or not, and gentle the pony for a few moments. Allow plenty of time—ponies can sense when anyone is in a hurry. They hate to be hustled.

Before putting on or taking off a halter always put the rope round the neck behind the pony's ears (Fig. 30), so that there is something to hold the pony by if it moves while the halter is being adjusted or removed.

A halter is better than a headcollar for catching up and turning out.

It may be necessary, as a temporary measure, to leave a head-collar (Fig. 31) on a pony at grass. It must be fitted very carefully.

Fig. 31.   Ample room for the jaws to move freely—use a brow band

It should admit of three fingers width anywhere round the nose so that there is ample room for the jaws to move freely when the pony eats. Always use a brow band (Figs. 31 & 35). It keeps the head collar in place, preventing it slipping back and rubbing the mane. The headcollar must be kept well oiled and soft to prevent chafing. Besides the possibility of chafing, there are other reasons against turning a pony out in a headcollar—the pony may get caught when rubbing against a tree or post, or it might get the heel of a shoe caught up in the leather when scratching its head with a hind foot.

Turning a pony out. It is the way a pony is turned out that often makes it difficult to catch up again. NEVER hustle a pony when turning it out (Fig. 32)—letting it gallop away immediately

Fig. 32.   NEVER hustle a pony when turning it out

does harm and may make it excitable when being turned out or caught up. Try to leave the pony before it moves. It is the last impression left on the pony's mind that counts.

Most ponies will soon learn the simple drill if care is taken each time. Shut the gate ; lead the pony at least ten yards into the field. Turn round and face the gate. Stand still ; pat the pony.

Take off its halter, pat the pony again and walk right away. If the pony must have a tit-bit give it just before walking away.

The reason for turning to face the gate is that if the pony does gallop away and kick one can get clear as it turns.

If more than one pony is being turned out keep well apart and arrange to let the ponies loose at the same moment.

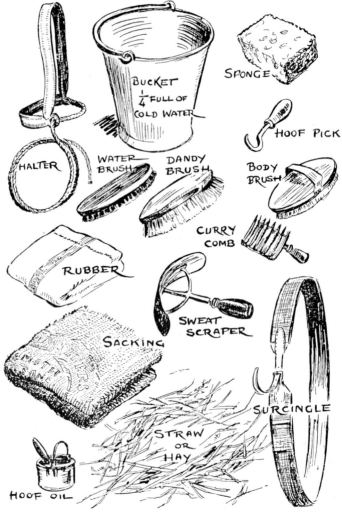

Fig. 33.   Things to have ready

CHAPTER 7

GROOMING

Things to have ready (Fig. 33) :

Halter ; bucket quarter full of cold water ; sponge, hoof pick, water brush, dandy brush, body brush and curry comb, rubber, sweat scraper, a large piece of sacking (a sack cut and opened out) a surcingle, a bundle of straw or hay ; hoof oil and brush. A set of stable bandages ; a tail bandage.

The grooming of a pony at grass is done to make the pony clean and tidy for the day's work, little or no grease being removed. It differs from that done to a stabled pony which is groomed to get out all grease, keep it really clean and healthy, and to tone up its muscles and circulation, because the pony is confined.

All healthy ponies at grass have a good natural shine on their coats. When ponies change their coats twice a year, Spring and Autumn, they do not want to be brushed too much. Nature's way being to shed a little, then grow a little.

Whether a pony is being groomed in the field, near the house, or in a shed or box, it must be tied up to something firm. The job cannot be done properly if the pony drifts and moves about. Remember to use a quick release knot (Fig. 34).

Grooming a dry pony. Sponge the eyes, nose and under the tail only if necessary. If overdone this removes too much natural grease. Pick out each foot. Using a water brush wash each foot, getting off the dry mud and dirt. There are two reasons for this— the feet and shoes can be properly inspected, and horn caked with old mud under a clean pony and tack spoils the turn out. So, even if the pony will get muddy again soon, wash the feet and try not to slosh water over the joints and pasterns. Practice makes for speed and efficiency.

Fig. 34. The pony must be tied up to something firm

Using a dandy brush get the mud off the body and legs. All the parts where the saddle, girth, martingale and bridle touch must be quite free from mud and dirt.

Use a body brush to do the mane and tail and do them both thoroughly. (The only time to use a comb is when plaiting or trimming). Putting on a tail bandage is optional depending on how soon the pony is going to be ridden. Remember to wet the tail only and never wet the bandage because it will shrink as it dries and get tight round the dock. Wipe the whole pony over the way of the hair with a rubber. Oil the feet, being careful to do all round the horn and across the bulbs of the heels.

Fig. 35. With a good handful of straw

Grooming a wet pony. Use a sweat scraper to get off the worst of the wet on the neck and body.

With a good handful of straw or hay rub the pony down getting off as much wet as possible (Fig. 35).

NEVER rub AGAINST the coat—that only rubs the wet in on to the skin. Always rub the way the coat lies.

A saddle must not be put on a wet back, so to help get the back really dry lay some fresh straw or hay all over the back and loins. Put on a piece of sacking to keep the straw in place, then put on a surcingle to prevent the sacking from sliding off (Fig. 36).

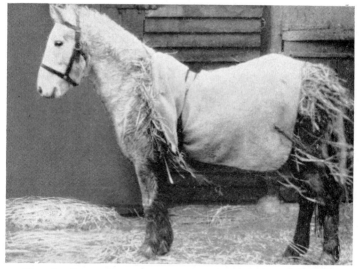

Fig. 36.   Do not leave a pony thatched much longer than an hour

With a rubber (or you can use straw) dry the ears thoroughly and pull them if they are cold.

Do the feet (the same as for grooming a dry pony).

Rub down legs and pasterns with a handful of straw or hay. If very muddy put on loosely a set of stable bandages with hay or straw underneath. The legs will dry quickly. Later the dry mud can be brushed off with a dandy brush.

Do the mane and tail, even if wet.

Give the pony some water and some hay or a feed, and leave it with the straw and sacking on for about an hour when it should be dry enough to have any mud brushed off and the grooming completed.

Do not leave a pony thatched with straw and sacking for much longer than an hour because it may get too hot and start to sweat and get itchy (Fig. 36).

A sack placed direct on a wet back will not dry it. Everything will just stay clammy and wet and the pony may catch cold. Putting straw under a sack allows the steam and damp air to get away, so that the pony dries off.

It is important, whether a wet or dry pony is being groomed, always to look it over for any hurt and to inspect the feet and shoes.

CHAPTER 8

CARE AFTER WORK

AFTER A SHORT RIDE—WHAT TO DO TO THE PONY

Ponies like to get back to their field directly after being worked. On the other hand after an ordinary ride it does a DRY pony no harm to put it in a stable. In the summer time it may be kept in for part of the day because of the flies.

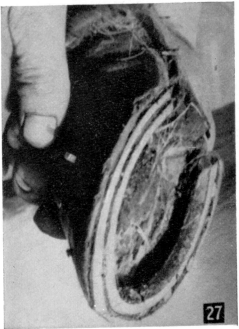

Fig. 37.   Inspect the shoes.   Shoe pressing into foot

Whichever is being done, give the pony a chance to stale then brush off the saddle mark and look the pony over for any hurt. Inspect the feet and shoes (Fig. 37).

AFTER A LONG DAY—WHAT TO DO TO THE PONY

The times that a pony must be put straight out into the field are after hunting, after a long day, or if the pony is wet with either rain or sweat. Any of these times, be it summer or winter, a grass kept pony should not be put in a stable, but be got into its field as soon as possible. These are not the times to dawdle and talk but to get on with doing what is necessary for the pony, which is : lead the pony into a box or somewhere sheltered from wind and rain in winter, or somewhere cool and shady in the summer.

Take off the saddle and bridle and put on a halter. Give the pony a chance to stale. Rub the saddle mark and behind the ears briskly with a handful of straw or hay to restore the circulation.

In winter offer some chilled water (that is tepid or slightly warm water) but do not worry or hang about waiting if the pony will not touch it.

Take a quick look round for any hurt—and then turn the pony out right away. Yes, even if it is pelting with rain or blowing a gale—most ponies go down and roll at once, have a good shake, pull a few mouthfuls of grass, go for a short trot and then have a drink. This is Nature's way of easing tired muscles, warming a pony up or drying itself off if sweating (Fig. 38).

In the meantime, if it is winter, the pony's feed and hay can be put out into its usual place in the field.

Treating a pony in this way will keep its feet, legs and wind right and will avoid chills and colds.

The next day after a long day. Without fail the following day the pony must be caught up and carefully looked over for cuts, thorns, sore mouth, back and girth galls or hurt of any sort. Brush off any remaining sweat marks.

Fig. 38.   Most ponies go down and roll at once

Pick out and look at the feet and shoes. There may be one or more clenches up (Figs. 26 & 39), or a loose or twisted shoe. Trot the pony up in hand on a road or on a level bit of hard ground to test for lameness.

Check that the pony did eat up its feed.

Turn the pony out again straight away, giving hay and feed as usual.

The pony will be better out in the field and not kept in a stable except in summer if the flies are bad.

It is only fair to the pony NOT to ride it the day after a hard or long day in summer or winter.

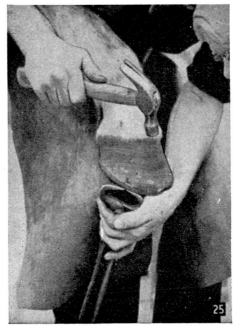

Fig. 39.   There may be one or more clenches up

CHAPTER 9

BRINGING A PONY INTO THE STABLE FOR A NIGHT

In very wet weather it is sometimes convenient to catch up the pony the night before a day's hunting.

The pony must be thoroughly dried, the feet picked out and washed and the mane and tail brushed. Follow the full details as for grooming a wet pony.

In the box there must be a good bed of straw or other bedding, a bucket full of water, a feed and some hay.

The top door of the box is better left open so that there is plenty of air. The window, too, may be better open if on the same side as the door. Avoid a cross draught.

Ponies do not catch cold out of doors in all weathers but once one brings a pony into a stable without plenty of air it may catch cold.

When the pony is quite dry it is all right to put on a thin light-weight rug and a roller—an unlined jute or even a summer sheet is enough. A covering over the back and loins is a good thing for some ponies. It is not always a fact that because a pony has a thick coat it will not feel cold in a stable.

The pony in a field is not cold because it can move about freely and there are no draughts, whereas the pony in a stable, say 10 feet by 12 feet, is unable to move about enough to keep its circulation going, nor can it get away from a draught which it will feel, but you may not realise is there. As with everything to do with any animal no hard and fast rule applies—the ponies vary and every stable is different.

HOW TO KNOW AND WHAT TO DO IF THE PONY IS TOO HOT OR TOO COLD

If, when the pony has stood in for, say, a couple of hours, its ears are cold and its coat is staring, then the pony is cold.

If it is sweating and its ears are cold then the pony has broken out into a cold sweat and the pony is cold.

If the pony is sweating and its ears are hot and the box feels fuggy and airless, then the pony is too hot.

In the first case, the pony being obviously cold, it may be a help to put on a lightweight rug which will stop the pony from standing cold all night. Make sure it has a good, deep bed.

When a pony breaks out in a cold sweat it may be wet or only slightly damp down each side of its neck and on each flank, but the pony must be made warm and dry again. A good rub down with a handful of straw, the ears pulled to warm them, and a short walk outside the box, if it is not raining, will dry the pony off. The putting on of a lightweight rug, when the pony is quite dry, may help and also prevent the pony breaking out again that night.

For the over hot pony, try to get some more air circulating round the box. If it is not raining lead the pony out in the air and walk it about to cool off. A fuggy box is a menace.

The only way to find out the best thing to do is by trial and error and observation of each particular pony. Some just hate standing in and fuss and fret all the time—others do not mind where they are. Ponies, unlike horses, vary enormously on how they react to being in a stable.

The next morning, the earlier the better, half fill the water bucket, give the pony a good feed and pick up the droppings.

Pick out the pony's feet. Brush off any dry mud and caked droppings. Brush the mane and tail. Wipe the pony over with a rubber. In other words, groom the pony as you would after catching it up dry out of the field.

Fig. 40.   Good forelock to protect the eyes from flies

CHAPTER 10

TRIMMING, WASHING, CLIPPING

The pony needs a good mane and a full tail for protection in winter and in summer, but this does not mean bedraggled and neglected. A good thick, even mane, not too short, will not lie sodden on the pony's neck. It dries out quicker and is easy to keep brushed out.

A good forelock helps to protect the eyes from flies in the summer (Fig. 40).

Fig. 41.   It does need the end banged

The tail needs little or no pulling for it must be good and full all the way down. It does need the end banged, i.e. squared off (Fig. 41). Too long a tail with the end trailing in the mud and the hocks

never dry, is a sorry sight. It is no help to the pony's comfort or
to its tail carriage, whereas the tail well off the ground will dry
out quicker and is much easier to brush out. In summer an
over-long tail will soon become a thin and wispy tail.

Both mane and tail trimmed once in November or December,
should keep in good shape throughout the winter when the hair
is growing very little. In spring and summer they may need some
trimming and tidying two or three times, according to how fast
the hair grows.

A well kept mane and tail are easy to plait at any time (Fig. 42).

Fig. 42.   Well kept mane is easy to plait

In winter a pony needs the fetlock and the hair down the back of
the pastern and heels for protection. But in the summer it
smartens a pony to have these trimmed.

With some ponies the old hairs of the fetlock and on the pastern
come out easily by plucking with thumb and finger, when the
pony is changing its coat. Otherwise it should be done with
scissors and comb which keeps the hair lying naturally. If done
with hand clippers it always shows and looks rough.

A pony uses its eyelashes and the whiskers on its muzzle as feelers in the dark. These should never be cut off—nor should the hair be cut from inside the ears because it is needed for protection against weather and flies.

Washing. Manes, tails and light coloured ponies. For a special occasion, and in warm weather it is quite all right to wash the mane and tail or the whole pony. Do not wash often because washing removes natural oil and grease which is the pony's protection against sun, flies, rain and wind. For the same reason use soap and NOT a detergent. Soap leaves a little natural grease whereas detergent removes too much.

When washing the whole pony do it in a corner out of the wind. Have everything you will need ready BEFORE you begin—use water that only just has the chill off. Never use hot water.

Put a halter on the pony. Tie it up or have someone to hold it. Have ready one bucket of tepid soap suds, a piece of soap and a sponge. Either a dipper or a small old saucepan with a handle are excellent for pouring the soapy water and the swilling water over the pony. Several pieces of turkish towelling for drying. Three buckets each two-thirds full of tepid water and one bucket of hot water. (This hot water is to add to the tepid water which chills rapidly. In this way the pony can be washed in water all the same temperature).

Wash the head only if you must and keep it as dry as possible taking great care not to let any soap get into the pony's ears and eyes. Then sponging and washing as you go do the neck, mane, and so on all over the pony's body, legs and tail. Use extra soap on very dirty patches and on the mane and tail. Rinse the pony over very thoroughly getting out all the soap. Use a sweat scraper on the neck and body to remove surplus soap and again after rinsing.

Speed with the drying process is important to prevent a chill. Dry the ears and loins really well (Fig. 43). Get off the worst of the

Fig. 43.   Speed with the drying process is important

wet from the rest of the body and legs. Get the pony on the move, leading it about in the sunshine (if any) but out of the wind, as soon as possible.

If there is difficulty in getting the pony quite dry put some hay or straw on the back and loins and put on a rug and roller. When the pony is absolutely dry and warm put on a summer sheet or light rug and a roller and put the pony in a stable with clean straw. He is sure to roll.

Clipping. Most ponies grow a heavy winter coat.

When worked, the pony sweats profusely and gets very thirsty. Unnecessary sweating makes a pony lose condition.

If a pony is clipped trace-high or has just its belly and one run up the wind pipe clipped out, it is a great help and the kindest thing to do if the pony is going to do any work in the winter (Fig. 44).

Fig. 44. NOT exaggerated. Low top line. Hair left on quarters and up round root of tail

Fig. 45   Clipped trace-high exaggerated up quarters and up gullet

When hunting or being ridden it will not feel its coat so much, will sweat less and will dry off quicker.

Ponies will come to no harm out at grass when clipped trace-high, providing the clip is not exaggerated by having too much coat removed along the sides and quarters, or up the gullet (Figs. 44 and 45). Once clipped should be enough. If it is done at the end of November or early December, then the pony will be accustomed to it by the time the very cold winds and weathe start —also, a certain amount, but not too much, coat will have grown again.

CHAPTER 11

NEW ZEALAND RUG

This is a blanket lined weatherproof rug with special fittings to prevent it from blowing about. It can be used on a clipped pony which is going to be ridden regularly throughout the winter. The pony can be clipped with a hunter clip (Fig. 47) and turned out in a New Zealand rug. One clip will be enough and it should be done in

Fig. 46. New Zealand Rug. Weatherproof with special fittings

November or early December. The pony will then get used to the loss of its coat and will have grown a small amount of coat before the severe weather and cold winds set in.

Careful attention must be paid to the following points :

1 The rug should be tried on and the pony gentled and led about a few times before it is needed for regular use. The straps come in unaccustomed places and may frighten a

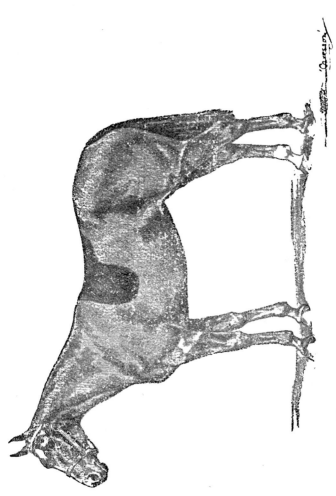

Fig. 47 A hunter clip and can be turned out in a New Zealand rug

pony if the rug is put on and the pony is turned out without some preparation.

2 The rug must be taken off and put on again carefully at least ONCE EVERY DAY. The ideal is to have two rugs —one on and one off. In this way all the straps can be kept well oiled. The rug can be properly dried, the blanket lining kept brushed and clean, and the whole rug kept in proper repair.

3 A watch must be kept where the rug fits closest for chafing and galling, and steps taken at once to check any hurt.

4 Never stand the pony in a stable in a New Zealand rug. Being waterproof it is thick and heavy and allows no air to the pony's body. It is like wearing your mackintosh indoors. Put on a jute or other rug when the clipped pony has to stand in.

5 After a day's hunting the pony must be turned out into its field as soon as possible (the detail for this is on page 45: "After a long day what to do with the pony"), but some extra care must be taken to get off mud where the rug, surcingle and straps touch to prevent chafing. Dry the back and loins first, then keep them covered with a couple of sacks or a rug, putting straw underneath if the back is still damp. Then do the rest of the pony—avoid letting the pony stand about and get cold. A clipped-out pony chills down very quickly. Finally, put on the New Zealand rug.

6 A pony clipped-out and turned out in a New Zealand rug needs a generous extra ration daily of warming and energy-making food (i.e. oats, beans, maize, horsenuts). It is important to remember that the rug is NOT a complete substitute for the pony's natural coat—therefore if the pony is to keep its condition, it must be given much more food to help it maintain its body warmth.

CHAPTER 12

MINOR AILMENTS AND FIRST AID

A pony at grass should be looked over daily for wounds or illness. Neglect of proper and immediate care may have serious consequences.

It is a good plan to have a definite method of running over the pony, doing it the same way each time, then nothing will get missed. Knowing a pony's habits is a help in spotting if anything is wrong, i.e. when and where it usually lies in the field, how and where it often stands, etc. Ponies are, as a rule, tough and hardy and certainly do not want pampering, but given a little thoughtful daily care they will work on happily for years. It is no credit to any pony owner if his or her pony is continually having things the matter with it and being unable to be worked. Do not blame the pony.

Medicine cupboard. The fewer things in it, the better. A number of jars and bottles with stale, once used contents are useless. What is needed is a minimum of clean necessities always available :

> A pair of scissors—blunt ended for choice.
> Cotton wool kept in a sponge bag.
> A sponge.
> A piece of good toilet soap in a soap tin.
> Roll of waterproof Elastoplast 1 inch wide.
> Elastoplast bandage $2\frac{1}{2}$ inches wide.
> Jar, with tight lid, of cooking salt.
> Zinc ointment and/or tube of Acriflavine cream
> Tin of Kaolin.
> Tin of dusting powder.
> Bottle of tincture of iodine

Cuts and wounds must be washed with clean cold water and dressed as soon as possible. If they are neglected flies will cause festering in the summer and mud will cause trouble in the winter.

To protect surface cuts and scratches, smear on plain Zinc ointments, Acriflavine cream or just dust with powder. Deep cuts and puncture wounds need skilled attention.

Lumps. There will be soreness and bruising with lumps with heat in them and with a cut from a blow, kick or tread. Use the garden hose to trickle cold water VERY GENTLY from well above, so that the water flows and spreads over the sore area (Fig. 48). Alternate with Kaolin applied as below :

If a **Thorn** is suspected bathe gently and frequently with warm water and smear warm Kaolin on a trimmed piece of greaseproof paper, using strips of elastoplast to hold it in place. It will stick on without a bandage providing the surrounding hair is dry.

Girth galls, wrung withers and sore backs need bathing with cold water with a little salt dissolved in it. If the skin is unbroken then dabbing two or three times a day with methylated spirit will harden them.

Insect stings anywhere on the body can cause big soft lumps which usually go down on their own in a few hours. If on the eyelid or near the eye a sting can be bathed VERY GENTLY with cold water or cold tea.

Avoid bandaging cuts or wounds unless given skilled advice to do so. Bandages rarely stay in place and this causes dressings to slip or rub. If bandages are tight they cause pressure and soreness and may restrict free circulation which will delay healing. If the hair is dry where a dressing is to be put on the pony's body, use waterproof Elastoplast, criss-crossed to hold the dressing in place. A short length of Elastoplast bandage is very good for holding a

Fig. 48.   Trickle cold water VERY GENTLY

dressing in place on a limb or joint. Being elastic it does not hamper movement or circulation, nor can the pony rub it off.

Avoid over-washing or any but the gentlest of washing of a cut or wound. The surrounding tissues are very fragile and are easily damaged, thus delaying healing. For the same reasons avoid the use of any but the mildest form of disinfectant, or use salt and water which both cleanses and helps healing. Remember a pony's skin cannot bear anything nearly so hot or so strong on it as we can bear and use on our own skin.

Lameness. May be noticed when the pony walks but more often when it trots. Examine each shoe and under each foot. FEEL for heat on feet and limbs.

For a suspected **kick** or **blow,** treatment is dealt with on page 62, under 'lumps.'

Very slight sprains, twists and wrenches will usually right themselves in a day or two if the pony is kept out in the field and not worked. Using the garden hose to trickle cold water over the area for twenty minutes two or three times a day will be a help.

Bad sprains need skilled attention.

There are many reasons for a pony being lame. It is not practical or possible to go into them all here. Skilled advice on the spot is necessary.

Usually a lame pony is better out in its field than standing in a stable getting stiff.

Avoid turning a lame pony sharply.

A lame pony must NOT be worked.

The application of either tincture of Arnica or plain goose grease will soon take the ache and soreness out of a blow, slight sprain, wrench or twist. They are old-fashioned remedies but are very effective and inexpensive.

Illness. A pony might become ill (Fig 49). One is able to recognise this as the pony will be standing with head down, ears back and its coat will be staring. It will be tucked up and looking thoroughly miserable.

The first thing to do is to lead the pony to a box or shed and send for the veterinary surgeon. In the meantime pull the pony's ears to warm them—they are sure to be cold. If the pony is wet rub it down, put some straw or hay, then a rug or blanket or sack over its

Fig. 49. Tucked up and looking thoroughly miserable

loins. Cover the back and loins with a rug or sack in any case. Offer the pony some hay. Put straw or bedding of some sort on the box floor.

Coughing must not pass unnoticed. It may be the first indication of trouble to come. It is wise to consult the veterinary surgeon before that trouble develops into something serious.

Out on a ride, if the pony gives an occasional dry-sounding cough it may be just a bit of dust or it wants to clear its wind. Notice if it coughs more than a couple of times.

If the cough is a wet, thick, gurgle-sounding one, and the pony is not breathing quite right—then seek advice.

If there is hardly any cough but the pony's nose is running—then seek advice.

Do not work a pony with a cough.

Whatever the cough, the pony is better out in the open air and not in a stable.

Ponies being over-ridden or galloped too much may develop a cough and may, in time, become broken-winded. This is because the stomach, being full of grass, presses on the diaphragm and restricts the expansion of the lungs which are already having difficulty to keep up with the too violent exercise.

Thinness may be caused by any of the following :

The pony not having enough to drink.
Not having enough to eat.
Not having enough bulk food.
Poor quality food.
Sharp teeth.
Worms.
Pony being bullied by other ponies.
Temperament.
Conformation.
An illness.

(The first four have already been dealt with under "Grazing and Feeding").

Teeth. The veterinary surgeon must be called in to advise. He will rasp them, if necessary.

Worms. If a pony has worms, red or other kinds, at all badly, it will never look big and well until the worms have been got rid of. Seek the advice of the veterinary surgeon. Worms will recur if the field does not have proper care. (See "Grazing and care of Grass").

Bullying. Sometimes a pony is bullied by others in the field. It never gets a chance to settle and graze—consequently it becomes worried and loses condition. The only remedy is to remove either it or the bully from the field.

Temperament of a pony that frets, fusses, sweats easily, breaks out or rarely seems relaxed when being worked. A pony of this type is not easy to keep big and well.

Conformation. The shape a pony is made cannot be altered. Short of a back rib ; a middle piece shaped like a drain pipe ; a ewe neck ; a rather high back bone ; split up between the hind legs ; sunken fundament ; a narrow-chested, mangy sort of pony ; any of these are bad conformation and are no help in keeping a pony in good condition all the year round.

Lice usually trouble ponies at grass in the spring. They can easily be seen if the hair of the mane or tail is parted. If allowed to infest the pony it will rub bare patches on its mane, tail, back, neck or withers. Ask a chemist for a good brand of lice powder and follow the directions on the packet.

Sweet itch. Chiefly affecting mountain and moorland types (as those in Figs. 2, 3, 9, 12, 17, 18, 20, 25 and 44) of ponies in spring and autumn, the pony rubbing the hair off its mane and tail. It is a very tiresome complaint, not unlike eczema in dogs, and very itchy. Being in the blood it can only be kept in check and not cured. Avoid rich grazing and any kind of food that might overheat the pony's blood. There are many soothing ointments and lotions apply externally.

Summer Laminitis. The pony's feet have the whole of its weight to carry so that if the pony is rather over-fat (Fig. 17) in the summer and it is trotted fast on roads or hard.ground then fever in the feet may result. There will be heat in the feet (usually the fore feet) and the pony showing signs of discomfort in the feet. Skilled advice must be sought. In the meantime have the shoes removed to ease pressure. Do not leave the pony standing in.

Ringworm. A small round bare patch the size of a shilling with a tiny brown speck in the middle. It may occur on any part of the pony. Being contagious it can easily be caught from other ponies or from cattle. Dab on iodine immediately and once daily. This will kill the ringworm.

If no more patches appear after five days, then the pony should be free and resume normal routine. Being so catching it is wiser not to take a pony with ringworm into a stable, groom it or touch it more than necessary—anything that has been near should be hung in the air and sun or disinfected.

Thrush. Dirt, and neglect of proper care of ponies' feet and thrush go hand in hand. A pony is not usually troubled with thrush if the feet are regularly picked out and the blacksmith is visited at proper intervals.

Thrush can be smelt when a pony's foot is lifted and picked out. The cleft of the frog becomes slimy. A chemist will supply a tin of Stockholm tar. Pick out and thoroughly wash the feet ; then with a short stiff brush paint Stockholm tar all over the heels, sole and frog, getting well into the cleft and grooves. This treatment must be done daily until the thrush is got rid of.

More information about these and other minor ailments may be found in "The Manual of Horsemanship".

CHAPTER 13

COMPANIONSHIP

It is kinder to turn out two ponies together. In the winter they protect each other. In the summer they stand head to tail to help keep off the flies (Figs. 10 and 50).

One pony turned out alone can be very lonely, and have a very bad time with the flies and, in the winter, with the wind and rain.

Fig. 50.   It is kinder to turn out two ponies together

CHAPTER 14

BRINGING IN A PONY IN SUMMER

Flies are worse in some districts and fields than in others. Ponies walk a tremendous distance in a day trying to avoid them ; also they will gallop if flies are very bad. To bring a pony into a cool airy box or shed for a few hours will save it a good deal of discomfort and much wear of its joints, feet and shoes.

The pony may be in the stable from about 10 a.m. till 5 p.m. which is a long time with no food. So give a small mid-day short feed or a small net of hay. Be sure there is always a bucketful of clean water in the box.

For the following two reasons (and there are others) there must be bedding on the box floor—not necessarily expensive straw ; any dry litter will do.

1. The pony will want to stale during the time it is in the stable. Few ponies will trust themselves to do this unless there is enough bedding to prevent them slipping.

2. If there is bedding the pony will lie down during the day, which is good for it. It will not have much time for rest when turned out in the evening because it will be busy eating. It is cruel to stand any pony for long in a stable with little or no bedding.

Treat the pony as a stabled pony for the time it is in, that is :
Keep the droppings picked up, the water bucket topped up and the box tidy.

After the pony is turned out in the evening, set the box fair so that it is all ready for the pony to come into the next day.

Ponies are conservative and sometimes shy drinkers. It may be that a pony will not always drink from a stable bucket. One must not be misled into thinking that the pony never drinks very much. Watch when it is turned out. It will either go straight to its usual drinking place, or after a roll and a mouthful of grass, trot off to drink (Fig. 38).

CHAPTER 15

RIDING A PONY OFF GRASS

Remember these three facts :

1. That although the pony's feet and legs get plenty of walking exercise they do not harden up—so ride on the side of a road or on the grass verge. Avoid the middle of the road or riding on a hard road unless absolutely necessary.

2. That the pony's back muscles, where it carries its saddle and its rider, get out of practice for carrying weight. The back and loins are where a pony gets tired. Therefore NEVER SIT ON ANY PONY UNNECESSARILY, nor for too long. When its back starts to get tired a pony may trip, brush, stumble, refuse to jump or not jump well, it may pull, and be blamed for all sorts of other things whereas the pony is only trying to ease tired muscles.

3. That the pony gets out of the habit of having a long day's work be it hunting, a working rally or a competition. The pony will get tired and thirsty even if its rider does not—many a pony, young and old, gets soured by continually giving of its best while its rider never knows when to call it a day. So always, when possible, at ALL convenient times, give the pony a short rest, a short drink at a trough or stream, and a few mouthfuls of grass, This does no harm and will go a long way in keeping the pony fresh and warding off fatigue.

So, briefly, to sum up the needs of the pony kept out to grass :

Fresh clean water always.
Shelter from flies and wet windy weather.
To be caught up and looked over every day.
A strong gate and good fences.
To visit the farrier every four to six weeks.
Hay every day from November to May.
A change of grazing.
Another pony for companionship.

I think that the pony kept out to grass being out of sight needs just as much care and forethought as that of the stabled pony which is continually under one's eye.

And in everything to do with ponies at all times these three words to remember :

ALERTNESS . ANTICIPATION . COURTESY

CHAPTER 16
RIDING ON ROADS, SIGNALS AND ROAD SENSE

The Highway Code applies to everybody using the roads, whether they are driving a car, or walking, or riding a pony or a bicycle.

THINGS TO KNOW WHEN RIDING OR LEADING A PONY IN THE ROAD :

Learn, from the Highway Code, the signals of other road users so that you know and understand what they intend to do.

It is very important to know how to signal what you intend to do and for other road users to understand you.

These are the Signals Riders must know and use :

(Figs. 51, 52, 53, 54).

Give the signals clearly using your whole arm.

Give them in PLENTY OF TIME. Vehicles cannot stop as quickly as a pony.

Practise putting the reins and stick in one hand in order to free the other hand and arm for signalling. Do this frequently off the roads so that you are absolutely signal-wise.

Be sure your pony can be led from his off side as well as his near side both dismounted and from another pony.

Do this off the road and practise giving signals when leading so that they are done easily without getting into a fuss or flap what to do. Practise often.

Try to avoid riding on main or busy roads.

Ridden or led ponies are not allowed on Motorways.

Now more details that all riders should know and understand :

Riding alone or in a small party

Look ahead and ride straight.

Keep well in to the left.

Ride in single file if the road is at all narrow or has bends.

Leader walk or jog at a steady pace to avoid the rear file having to trot up fast.

Look both ways before moving off, turning or halting.

If trotting, go steadily round all corners.

Have your reins short enough for your pony to be really under control.

Obey police, traffic control signals and traffic lights.

Give way to pedestrians at Zebra Crossings.

Look behind and in front before you pull out to pass a stationary vehicle, to make sure the road is clear.

It is NOT your road when a vehicle is stationary in front of you on your side of the road, i.e., a vehicle or person coming towards you has the right of way.

Ride on the grass verge where possible (some local councils forbid it).

In a built-up area be considerate for mown grass in front of houses and elsewhere.

If your pony shies, turn his head away from the object and DON'T LOOK AT IT YOURSELF.

You need not ride in silence BUT keep alert to road conditions.

Riding in a party of more than four :

Never ride more than two abreast.

Decide at once who will drop back to form single file when necessary.

Divide into columns of four or five.

Leave 100 yards at least between each column.

Put a steady pony in the lead.

Have beginners and/or small ponies in the middle.

NALS

se are the signals you should know and use.
them clearly with your whole arm.

I am
going to
TURN LEFT

Fig. 51.

I am
going to
TURN RIGHT

Fig. 52.

PLEASE
STOP

Fig. 53.

I am
going to
SLOW DOWN
or **STOP**

Fig. 54.

for the safety of all concerned, you
k it necessary for a motorist to
, slow down or give you more room,
should endeavour to make this clear
ignalling like this.

Leading and rear files make clear signals.

Leader set the pace. Keep it slow to avoid trotting or canter-
ing up of the rear files.

Have nervous or traffic-shy ponies on the inside.

Crossing a main road or at a road junction :

At a main road or at road junctions, look right, then left, then
right again before crossing or emerging. If the road is clear,
walk quickly and straight across. If it is not, wait quietly, be
alert and do not fidget.

If in a party, never start to cross a road until all the riders are
near enough to cross together. Wait until the road is clear
enough to allow the whole party to cross in safety.

NEVER GET SEPARATED — some on one side of the road
and some on the other.

Riding or leading at night :

Take special care on the road at night, in twilight or in fog and
mist.

Carry a light which shows white in front and red to the rear —
one specially made for attaching to the off-side stirrup is
best. It is called a stirrup lamp and can be bought at most
saddlers.

Whether you have a light or not, tie something white, a hand-
kerchief or rag, to your offside arm or stirrup. Better still
use a strip of reflective material obtainable from most
garages and wear it as low as possible round the ankles or
heels.

A reflective band which can be worn on arm or leg helps to
make you visible at night. These may be obtained, price
10p, from The Royal Society for the Prevention of Accidents,
52 Grosvenor Gardens, London, S.W.1.

The leader of a large party should carry a white light and the
rearmost rider a red one.

Leading :

> If leading another pony when mounted, have it on your near side and conform with other road users by riding on the left side of the road.
>
> When leading on foot, always place yourself between your pony and the traffic whether you are on the right hand or left hand side of the road.
>
> Be careful when passing pedestrians, particularly if your pony is difficult.
>
> Pat your pony and speak to him if he is nervous of high vehicles.
>
> Look ahead and walk straight.

Riding or leading on a slippery road :

> Get off it as soon as possible.
>
> Trust your pony and let him walk on.
>
> He does not want to fall. If you leave him alone he is less likely to slip.
>
> On icy roads quit your stirrups.
>
> If your pony falls, pick yourself up and let him get up. Pat him.
>
> Do not try to mount where it is still slippery.
>
> If leading, do not try to pull your pony along. Hook the end of the reins over your arm and walk on. He will follow. Concentrate on keeping your own feet.

Snow:

> Stop at a garage or farm. Ask for THICK motor grease. Smear thickly on soles and frogs on all four feet. The snow will then not ball. If going far, do this more than once.

Insurance :

> It is advisable for every rider and pony owner to hold some form of Third Party Legal Liability Insurance. The rider might be considered liable if his pony were to break loose or

cause any damage to other people or their property. For particulars of Insurance write to the British Horse Society, National Equestrian Centre, Kenilworth, Warwickshire, CV8 2LR

Be Courteous :

Be considerate and help others on the road.

Acknowledge the courtesy of other road users with a gesture and a smile.

Pass others at a walk on a bridle path or narrow road.

Fig. 55.

Pass at a walk on narrow roads

These three words to remember :

ALERTNESS — ANTICIPATION — COURTESY

They are the Keynote to safe and happy riding on the roads.

INDEX